Face-to-Face
with
The Hamster

Text and photos by
Paul Starosta

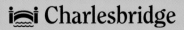 Charlesbridge

A hamster's cage door should be shut
and locked so the hamster cannot escape.

A quick getaway

It is nighttime. The room is quiet. A cage door opens, and a little hamster peeks out the door. The hamster sniffs the air, checking for danger. Before the hamster can escape, its owner closes the cage door. The owner knows that once a hamster gets loose, it can be hard to find. Hamsters are small enough to hide in closets or squeeze into mouse holes.

night life

Hamsters are nocturnal, meaning they are active at night. When they are awake, hamsters are lively and keep busy in their cages.

Hamsters have long whiskers that help them feel obstacles in the dark.

Weighing about 4 ounces, hamsters are so light that they don't even move the keys on a piano.

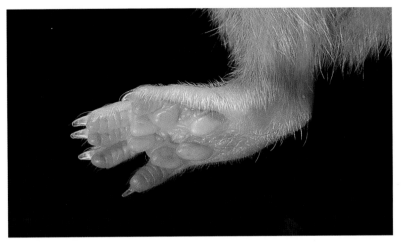

Hamsters have 5 toes on their back feet and 4 on their front feet. All their toes have claws.

A hamster's tail measures about half an inch long.

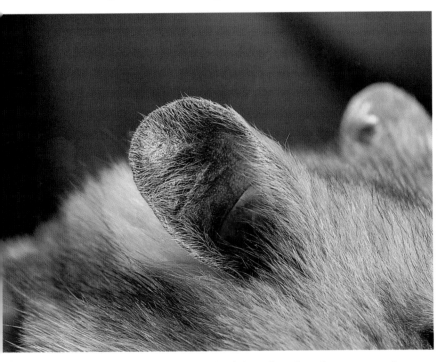

When its ears are folded back, the hamster is alert to danger.

Hamsters cannot see very well, but they have great senses of smell and hearing. They get around easily. With their clawed and padded feet, hamsters are well equipped for climbing. They also use their feet to hold food.

5

Gnawing a piece of spaghetti is no problem for a hamster.

The hamster uses its upper teeth to cut up the spaghetti.

The hamster stores the pieces in its cheek pouches.

Gnawing

Like all rodents, hamsters have two pairs of incisor teeth, one pair on the top and one pair on the bottom. These incisors are always growing, so hamsters have to keep using them. If a hamster does not keep gnawing, then its teeth will grow so large that it will not be able to close its mouth. Since hamsters will chew on anything, owners should keep hamsters away from dangerous objects like wires.

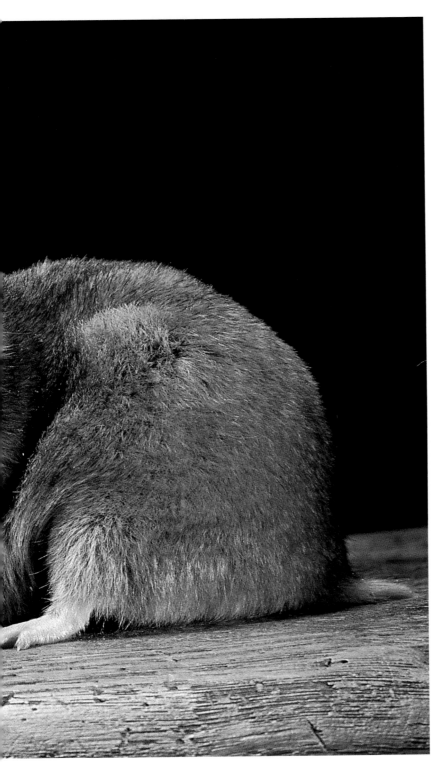

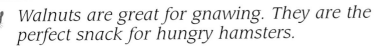 *Walnuts are great for gnawing. They are the perfect snack for hungry hamsters.*

In the pouch

Hamsters have two large pouches inside their mouth, one in each cheek. They use their cheek pouches to store food.

Before it stores the chestnut in its cheek pouches, the hamster peels off the shell.

Hamsters also eat fruits, vegetables, and meats.

🐾 *Hamsters store food so they will have something to eat if food becomes scarce.*

🐾 *In order to empty their pouches, hamsters push on their cheeks with their front feet.*

Hamsters cut their food into small pieces with their teeth and then stuff the pieces in their pouches. The more food they store, the fatter their cheeks get. When they get hungry, hamsters empty their pouches and eat.

9

Using its front feet like hands, a hamster can easily climb a ladder.

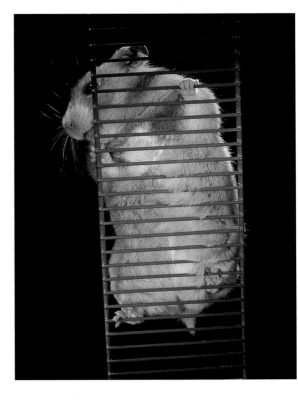

Hamsters have a great sense of balance, allowing them to descend a wheel headfirst.

There are many toys available that can keep a hamster busy exploring for hours.

Exercise

Hamsters need exercise and should have a variety of toys for this purpose. Exercise wheels, ladders, and tunnels keep hamsters occupied in their cages. Pet owners can also set up a safe play area outside the cage called a run. A hamster run should be bordered on all sides to prevent a hamster from escaping.

Hamsters are acrobatic. They can hang from a bar like a monkey.

Escape

Sometimes hamsters escape. They are curious and can slip out a half-opened door. It is dangerous for hamsters to roam around a house or outdoors. Loose hamsters can get stuck in a tight spot or attacked by an animal. Owners must be responsible by remembering to close cage doors and by keeping an eye on their hamster when it is outside of its cage.

Cats prey on small rodents such as hamsters. It is a good idea to keep these pets apart.

Outside, hamsters can fall prey to dogs, birds, or other animals.

Lost hamsters may become frightened. To calm a lost hamster, pick it up by holding it securely around its stomach.

13

🐹 *During the day hamsters sleep. They curl up in a ball to stay warm.*

🐹 *This curious hamster is checking out its surroundings.*

Mating ritual

Usually hamsters are solitary animals, meaning they live alone. At two months old, however, female hamsters are ready to have babies. Male and female hamsters share a cage so they can mate. Once they mate the pair can stay together until the female becomes aggressive toward the male. Then they are returned to their separate cages.

Hamsters groom their fur many times a day. They also groom to comfort themselves.

The male hamster is on the left. Males have larger hindquarters than females.

Pups are born

The female makes a soft nest for her babies out of cloth, straw, tissues, and other materials that she finds.

The mother has 12 teats. She can nurse all her newborn pups at the same time.

Within 5 days colored patches appear on the pups' skin.

When they are 10 days old, pups are covered in fur, but their eyes will not open for another 3 or 4 days.

At about 3 to 5 weeks old, hamsters are finished nursing. They are ready to leave the nest.

Sixteen days after mating, the female gives birth to several babies, called pups. Pups are born hairless and blind. They each weigh less than an ounce and measure about an inch long.

On their own

A month later, pups are lively and agile. They have separated from their mother, who will not take care of them anymore.
Instead, the pups play with one another and explore the world around them. They are now old enough to be handled by humans.

This pup is big enough to climb on its own.

After 2 months hamsters are adults. They are ready to leave the family cage and lead solitary lives.

With a lot of work, hamsters can be tamed in a few days.

The pups do not live together for long. Soon they start to fight one another. It is time for each pup to have its own cage. Each young hamster will need a responsible owner who will know how to train, tame, and play with it. If they are well cared for, hamsters can live to be four years old.

cages

Hamster care

Hamsters are easy pets to raise. They have pleasant natures and can be tamed with little trouble. Hamsters should be fed once a day. They also need plenty of exercise both in and out of their cages.

A hamster's **cage** should be spacious and kept inside, away from sunlight and out of the cold. When buying a cage, make sure the doors are secure. The cage needs to be cleaned every week, and wood shavings and bedding should be replaced.

exercise wheels

Hamsters can run up to two miles a night on their **exercise wheels**. Wire wheels are fine, but solid wheels ensure that a hamster's foot does not get caught between the rungs.

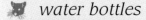

hamster houses

water bottles

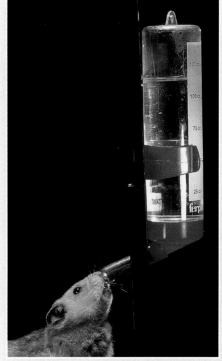

A **water bottle** allows a hamster to drink whenever it needs to. Water should be changed daily so that it is fresh.

A **hamster house** is a place for a hamster to nest. It can be made of stone, wood, or plastic. A hamster house is not necessary. Hamsters can also build a nest out of socks, shredded paper, or paper towels.

Hamster food is available in pet stores. As a treat, give a hamster a little bit of cheese or a piece of a fruit or vegetable.

Like humans, hamsters need to get out for a little **"recess."** Playing outside its cage helps keep a hamster cheerful.

recess

hamster food

Our worst enemies

Rodents are not well liked by people. They attack crops and sometimes transmit diseases to humans. But rodents are important as a source of food for predators such as birds and meat-eating animals.

A wild cousin

European hamsters, also called common hamsters, live in Eastern Europe. They are not raised as pets because they have nasty tempers. European hamsters can be found in the wild where they dig burrows. They are an endangered species, but many European governments are taking measures to protect European hamsters from extinction.

A European hamster in the wild.

22

Golden hamsters were discovered in semi-desert areas in Syria.

All one family

In 1930, Israel Aharoni, a scientist from the University of Jerusalem, made an expedition to Syria. In a region that was mainly desert, he came upon a female hamster and her 11 pups. He brought the hamsters back, and a colleague bred them. The offspring were sent to laboratories in America and Europe. All domesticated golden hamsters are descendants of this family.

Used for research

Because hamsters, mice, rats, and guinea pigs are easy to raise and reproduce, scientists use these rodents in laboratories. Scientists use rodents to test new medicines and make advances in scientific research.

White mice are used in experiments.

23

Other pets

All hamsters are part of the Rodentia order. Out of the 20 or so species of hamsters, only five have pleasant enough tempers to be suitable as pets. Other small animals from the Rodentia and Lagomorpha orders can also be raised as pets.

gerbils

Of the 80 species of **gerbils**, Mongolian gerbils are the easiest to tame, as long as you get one when it is young. They are very lively, can jump amazing distances, and stay awake during the day. Mongolian gerbils get along well with other pets.

rats

Rats are intelligent, not too timid, and can even be affectionate. They are also playful and seldom bite. Easy to tame, to feed, and to house, rats make ideal pets.

24

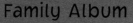
 rabbits

 *chinchillas*

Rabbits were once members of the order Rodentia, but were switched to the order Lagomorpha. Dwarf rabbits need toys to keep them busy. If they get bored, dwarf rabbits will start chewing things.

Chinchillas are great house pets if tamed at an early age. They are curious and intelligent animals. Chinchillas can live for 15 to 20 years.

Guinea pigs are gentle animals that like company and squeak if they are left alone too long. They are wonderful pets since they are not prone to disease and have very little odor. Their life expectancy is around five years.

guinea pigs

25

You'll find the answers to these questions about hamsters in your book.

Index

Photograph credits:

All photos taken by Paul Starosta except:
BIOS Agency: D. Halleux: p. 16 (top), p. 17 (top); N. Therond: p. 17 (bottom), p. 20 (bottom); J.-L. Klein and M.-L. Hubert: p. 20 (top), p. 21 (top left); R. Krekels/Fotonatura: p. 22 (bottom); D. Bringard: p. 23 (bottom)

COLIBRI Agency: A. Guerrier: p. 21 (bottom right); C. Testu: p. 24 (bottom), p. 25 (top left); A.-M. Loubsens: p. 25 (top right); J. Depech: p. 25 (bottom)

Milan/D. Chauvet: pp. 22–23 (top)

© 2004 by Charlesbridge Publishing. Translated by Elizabeth Uhlig.

© 2003 by Editions Milan under the title *Le Hamster*
300 rue Léon-Joulin, 31101 Toulouse Cedex 9, France
French series editor, Valérie Tracqui

Published by Charlesbridge
85 Main Street, Watertown, MA 02472
(617) 926-0329 • www.charlesbridge.com

Library of Congress Cataloging-in-Publication Data
Starosta, Paul.
[Hamster. English]
Face-to-face with the hamster / text and photos by Paul Starosta.
p. cm. — (Face-to-face)
Summary: Simple text explains the life cycle and care of hamsters.
ISBN 1-57091-456-7 (hardcover)
1. Hamsters as pets— Juvenile literature. [1. Hamsters. 2. Pets.]
I. Title. II. Face-to-face (Watertown, Mass.)
SF459.H3S7313 2004
636.935'6— dc22 2003020662

Printed in Singapore
10 9 8 7 6 5 4 3 2 1